Revised and Updated

T0080549

Communities

by Sarah L. Schuette

Consulting Editor: Gail Saunders-Smith, PhD

Mankato, Minnesota

Pebble Books are published by Capstone Press,
1710 Roe Crest Drive, North Mankato, Minnesota 56003.
www.capstonepub.com

Copyright © 2009 by Capstone Press, a Capstone imprint. All rights reserved. No part of this publication may be reproduced in whole or in part, or stored in a retrieval system, or transmitted in any form or by any means, electronic, mechanical, photocopying, recording, or otherwise, without written permission of the publisher.
For information regarding permission, write to Capstone Press,
1710 Roe Crest Drive, North Mankato, Minnesota 56003.

Library of Congress Cataloging-in-Publication Data
Schuette, Sarah L., 1976–
Communities / by Sarah L. Schuette. — Rev. and updated ed.
p. cm. — (Pebble books. People)
Includes bibliographical references and index.
Summary: "In simple text and photos, presents communities and the people who live in them"— Provided by publisher.
ISBN-13: 978-1-4296-2238-7 (hardcover)
ISBN-10: 1-4296-2238-5 (hardcover)
ISBN-13: 978-1-4296-3461-8 (softcover)
ISBN-10: 1-4296-3461-8 (softcover)
1. Communities — Juvenile literature. 2. Neighborhood — Juvenile literature. I. Title. II. Series
HM756.S38 2009
307 — dc22 2008026949

Note to Parents and Teachers

The People set supports national social studies standards related to individual development and identity. This book describes and illustrates communities. The images support early readers in understanding the text. The repetition of words and phrases helps early readers learn new words. This book also introduces early readers to subject-specific vocabulary words, which are defined in the Glossary section. Early readers may need assistance to read some words and to use the Table of Contents, Glossary, Read More, Internet Sites, and Index sections of the book.

Printed in the United States 5657

Table of Contents

What's a Community? 5
Living in a Community. 9
Working 15
A Nice Place. 21

Glossary 22
Read More 23
Internet Sites. 23
Index 24

What's a Community?

A community is a group of people who live in the same area.

BFGoodrich
Radial T/A

Communities can be
big or small.
A neighborhood, town,
or city can be a community.

Living in a Community

Community members
take care of each other
and where they live.

Ivan waters the flowers
in his yard.

Sally picks up garbage
on the sidewalk.

Weight: 0.00lb
$3.75
BALANCE $3.75
Kovle's
Market
Whole Grain
Kid-Tested
3g
110
KEMP'S
Select
JUICE
Large
White • Grade A

Working

People have many jobs
in communities.
Kevin works
at a grocery store.

Linda works
at the police station.
She directs traffic.

Hayes is a doctor.

He gives exams.

A Nice Place

A community is
a nice place to live.

Glossary

community — a group of people who live in the same area or who have something in common with each other

direct — to show or tell someone the way to go

neighborhood — the local area around your house

town — a group of neighborhoods that forms a community

Read More

Bodden, Valerie. *A Town.* My First Look at Communities. Mankato, Minn.: Creative Education, 2008.

Gillis, Jennifer Blizin. *Neighborhood Helpers.* My Neighborhood. Vero Beach, Fla.: Rourke, 2007.

Internet Sites

FactHound offers a safe, fun way to find educator-approved Internet sites related to this book.

Here's what you do:

1. Visit *www.facthound.com*
2. Choose your grade level.
3. Begin your search.

This book's ID number is 9781429622387.

FactHound will fetch the best sites for you!

Index

cities, 7
doctors, 19
exams, 19
garbage, 13
grocery stores, 15
jobs, 15
neighborhoods, 7
police station, 17
sidewalk, 13
towns, 7
traffic, 17
watering, 11
working, 15, 17
yards, 11

Word Count: 89
Grade: 1
Early-Intervention Level: 12

Credits
Kim Brown, cover designer; Abbey Fitzgerald, book designer; Marcy Morin, photo shoot scheduler

Photo Credits
Capstone Press/Karon Dubke, all

The author dedicates this book to her friends Dan and Suzanne Buck, of Henderson, Minnesota.